The Big Map

By Sally Cowan

Dad and I see the big map.

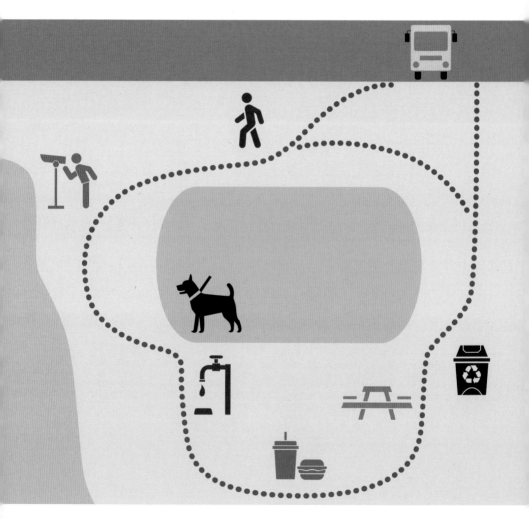

The big map has dots on it.

It has a red man.

I can jog.

man

dots

I can run up!

Dad can jog up.

At the top, I see a big jet.

jet

Dad and I met Jen.

Jen has a dog.

Her dog sips at the tap.

tap

dog

Dad got hot jam buns!

Dad got big cups.

I sat in the sun.

jam buns

The cups go in the big bin.

bin

Dad and I got on the big bus.

bus

I had fun!

CHECKING FOR MEANING

1. Where did Jen's dog have a drink? *(Literal)*

2. What did Dad and the boy have to eat? *(Literal)*

3. What are the symbols on the map for? *(Inferential)*

EXTENDING VOCABULARY

jet	What is a *jet*? What is another word that means the same thing as *jet*? If you took away the *j*, what other letter could you put at the start to make a new word? E.g. bet, let, met, net, pet, set.
hot	What sound is made by the letter *o* in the word *hot*? Can you find other words in the text where *o* makes the same sound?
buns	What are *buns*? When do we eat buns? What do we put inside the buns to make them taste good?

MOVING BEYOND THE TEXT

1. What places could you go where you would need a map?

2. What are some different types of maps?

3. What information can we find on a map?

4. Why do some cars have maps inside them?

SPEED SOUNDS

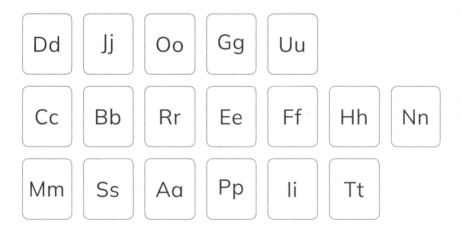

Dd	Jj	Oo	Gg	Uu
Cc	Bb	Rr	Ee	Ff	Hh	Nn
Mm	Ss	Aa	Pp	Ii	Tt

PRACTICE WORDS

Dad

big

dots

on

red

jog

run

up

top

jet

jam

dog

Jen

got

buns

sun

hot

cups

had

bus

fun

and